Super Cheap New York Travel Guide 2019

Our Mission

Travel guides show you pricey accommodation and restaurants because they make money OFF OF YOU. Travel bloggers and influencers often do the same. Super Cheap Guides help you use the system against itself to experience unforgettable trips that will blow your mind, not your budget.

We believe that travel can and is best enjoyed on a budget. We work to dispel myths, save you tons of money and help you find experiences that will flash before your eyes when you come to take your last breath on this beautiful earth.

Perhaps the biggest money saving trick you can employ is to know what you want to spend on and what you don't. This guide focuses on the cheap or free, but we do include the unique things to experience in our worth the fee section. There is little value in travelling somewhere and not experiencing all it has to offer. Where possible we've included cheap workarounds.

We are the first travel guide company to include Airbnb's in our recommendations if you think any of these need updating you can email me at philgtang@gmail.com

Who this book is for and why anyone can enjoy budget travel

Friends and family always ask me 'How can you afford to travel?' my response 'I have a unique skill and passion for finding bargains'. This doesn't mean I do any less or sleep in dirty hostels. Someone who spends A LOT on travel hasn't planned or wants to spend their money. I have formulated a system - which I hope to pass on to you in my travel guides - to juice everything from my travel adventures while spending the least possible money.

There is a difference between being cheap and frugal - I like to spend money on beautiful experiences, but 18 years of travel has taught me I could have a 20 cent experience that will stir my soul more than a $100 one. Of course, there are times when the reverse is true, my point is, spending money on travel is the best investment you can make but it doesn't have to be at levels set by hotels and attractions with massive ad spends and influencers who are paid small fortunes to get you to buy into something that you could have for a fraction of the cost.

Talking of 'the gram'. I've never used it, and probably never will though I have many friends who text me when they find good discounts on it or Twitter/Facebook, I love travelling so much because it forces me to be present-minded. I like to have the cold hard budget busting facts to hand (which is why I've included so many one page charts), but otherwise, I want to shape my own experience - and I'm sure you do too.

I have designed these travel guides to give you a unique planning tool to experience a soul-stirring trip without spending the ascribed tourist budget.

When it comes to FUN budget travel, it's all about what you know. You can have all the feels without most of the bills. An hour spent planning can save you hundreds on the same, maybe even thousands on the same experiences. Super Cheap Insider Guideshave done the planning for you, so you can focus on what matters: immersing yourself in the sights, sounds and smells, meeting awesome people and most importantly, being relaxed and happy. My sincere hope is that my tips will bring you great joy at a fraction of the price most people recommend.

So, grab a cup of tea, put your feet up and relax; you're about to enter the world of enjoying New York on the cheap. Oh and don't forget a biscuit. You need energy to plan a trip of a lifetime on a budget.

Super Cheap New York is <u>not</u> for travellers with the following needs:

1. You require a book with detailed offline travel maps. Super Cheap Guides are best used with Google Maps - download before you travel to make the most of your time and money.
2. You would like thousands of accommodation, food and attraction recommendations; by definition, cheapest is most often singular. We only include maximum value recommendations. We purposively leave out over-priced attractions when there is no workaround.
3. You would like detailed write-ups about hotels/Airbnbs/Restaurants. We are bargain hunters first and foremost. We dedicate our time to finding the best deals, not writing flowery language about their interiors. Plus things change. If I had a pound for every time I read a Lonely Planet description only to find the place totally different, I would be a rich man. Always look at online reviews for the latest up to date information.

If you want to save A LOT of money while comfortably enjoying an unforgettable trip to New York, minus the marketing, hype, scams and tourist traps read on.

Congratulations, you're saving money and doing Good!

We donate 10% of all book profits to charity. This year we are donating to Animal Shelters including one in New York.

The number of abandoned and homeless pets in America is estimated to be around 70 million. I'm sure you've seen your fair share of abandoned dogs during your travels: its heart wrenching to see man's best friend starving and alone.

'My dog Gracie was abandoned on the highway in Slovakia. At just ten months old, they tied her to the railings and left her there. Animal Hope picked her up and took care of her and found her a home with us. She is now a healthy, happy girl and loves travelling with us, getting her nose into new smells and soliciting belly rubs from fellow travellers. What breaks my heart is her 'I haven't been abandoned dance'. She is always so happy that we haven't abandoned her when we collect her from outside a supermarket that she dances on her leash for several minutes. Watch her 'I haven't been abandoned dance' dance   . Money could never buy the happiness she has brought my family and me, but donations can help other abandoned animals like her to find loving homes.'

Katherine Huber, a contributor to Super Cheap Vienna.

Donations are made on the 4th January of each year on profits from the previous year. To nominate a charity to receive 10% of the proceeds of sales from our 2020 editions complete the form here: supercheapinsiderguides.com

Gracie

Redefining Super Cheap

I grew up thinking you had to spend more than you could afford to have a good time travelling. Now I've visited many countries I know nothing is further from the truth. Before you embark upon reading our specific tips for New York. I want you to think about what you associate with the word cheap because you make your beliefs and your beliefs make you.

Here are the dictionary definitions of cheap:

1. costing very little; relatively low in price; inexpensive:
a cheap dress.
2. costing little labor or trouble:
Words are cheap.
3. charging low prices:
a very cheap store.
4. **of little account; of small value; mean; shoddy:**
cheap conduct; cheap workmanship.
5. **embarrassed; sheepish:**
He felt cheap about his mistake.
6. **stingy; miserly:**
He's too cheap to buy his own brother a cup of coffee.

Three out of six definitions have extremely negative connotations. The 'super cheap' we're talking about in this book is not shoddy, embarrassed or stingy. Hey, you've already donated to charity just by buying this book - how is that stingy? We added the super to reinforce our message. Super's dictionary definition stands for 'a super quality'. Super Cheap stands for enjoying the best on the lowest budget. Question other peoples definitions of cheap so you're not blinded to possibilities, potential, and prosperity. Here are some new associations to consider forging:

Shoddy

Cheap stuff doesn't last is an adage marketing companies have drilled into consumers. However by asking vendors the right questions cheap doesn't mean something won't last, I had a $10 backpack last for 8 years and a $100 suitcase bust on the first journey. A   out of San Francisco University found that people who spent money on experiences rather than things were happier. Memories last forever, not things, even expensive things. And as we will show you during this guide you don't need to pay to create great memories.

Embarrassed

I have friends who routinely pay more to vendors because they think their money is putting food on this person's table. Paradoxically, Cuban doctors are driving taxi's because they earn more money; it's not always a good thing for the place you're visiting to pay more and can cause unwanted distortion in their culture - Airbnb pushing out renters is an obvious example. Think carefully about whether the extra money is helping people or incentivising greed.

Stingy

Cheap can be eco-friendly. Buying thrift clothes is cheap but you also help the Earth. Many travellers are often disillusioned by the reality of traveling experience since the places on our bucketlists are overcrowded. Cheap can take you away from the crowds. You can find balance and harmony being cheap. Remember, "A journey is best measured in friends, rather than miles." – Tim Cahill. And making friends is free!

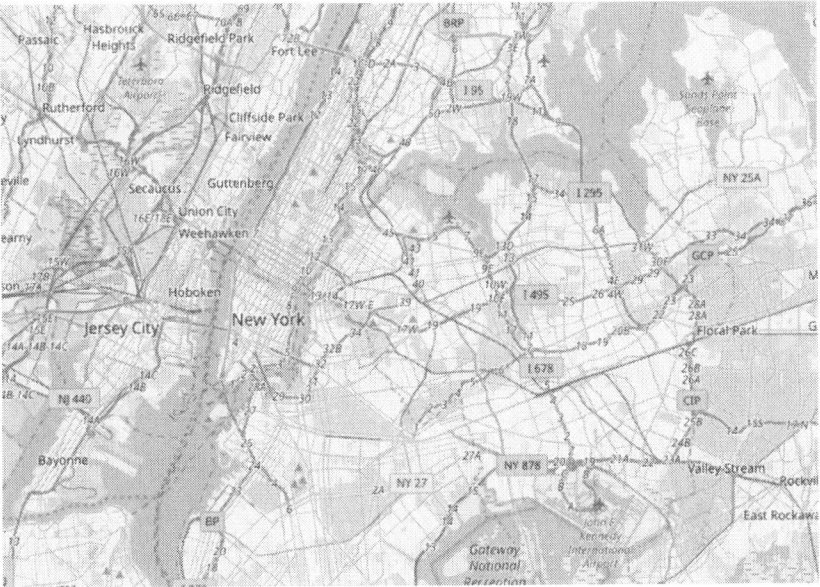

Discover New York

New York was founded by the Dutch in 1624 they named it 'New Amsterdam'. In 1664 the British took control and renamed it New York. Today New York is just like it is in the movies: horns honked by yellow cab drivers, street corners inhabited by hot dog vendors and fashionata's walk the streets Sex and The City style. The first time you walk around Times Square you will wonder if you are in a New York movie.

8.6 million people call the largest city in the USA home among them 78 billionaires. New York is made up of five boroughs: Manhattan, The Bronx, Queens, Brooklyn, and Staten Island. Despite the Billionaires, New York offers a wealth of opportunities to experience the city for free or cheap, from strolls through the city streets marvelling at the skyscrapers to free museums, exhibitions, public buildings, parks and churches, as well as fabulous cheap eats in Chinatown, Little Italy and Soho. There's so much to see and do that you will be planning your second visit.

Like any city that caters to tourists New York can quickly empty your wallet but take heart, the trick to keeping your trip affordable is to get off the tourist track and find the local deals. Use this guide to make sure New York leaves a lasting impression on your heart and mind, not your bank balance.

If you follow the advice in this guide you could definitely get away with spending about $40 a day including accommodation.

Planning your trip

When to visit

If you are not tied to school holidays, the best time to visit is during the shoulder-season months April to June and September to early November when the weather is warmer but the tourist crowds are fewer. The cheapest time to visit New York is on weekends from mid-January to the end of February but winter weather can be extreme.

Key dates

January - Martin Luther King Jr Day Every year on the third Monday of January a parade between 61st and 86th St. on 5th Avenue commemorates the famous civil rights activist.

March - St Patrick's Day Parade New York is famous for its St Patrick's Day parade which is the world's largest outside Ireland. Book your spot on Fifth Ave for the best view.

April - Tartan Day Parade Over 10,000 pipers and drummers congregate on 6th Ave to celebrate their Scottish roots for this annual parade.

May - Ninth Avenue Food Festival Just two blocks west of Times Square in Hell's Kitchen, this food festival attracts a million people who come to sample culinary delights from all over the world.

June - Museum Mile Festival For one day in June NYC's Museum Mile becomes one big block party. There's live music and lots more.

July - Independence Day On July 4th a huge fireworks display takes place over the East River. To make sure you witness it, you just have to make sure you get a spot close to the river!

August - Blues, Barbecue and Fireworks Festival Enjoy free music, barbecued food and a huge fireworks display at this one-day festival as part of the Hudson River Park's 'Summer of Fun'.

September - San Gennaro Festival Little Italy becomes awash with activity for this annual festival which takes place on Mulberry St. Sample various culinary delights, and if you're not hungry, play various games at different stalls.

October - Oktoberfest Munich isn't the only city where Oktoberfest is celebrated - New York gets in on the act also! Third Ave closes and drinking, eating, dancing, and everything German is celebrated.

November - Macy's Thanksgiving Day Parade This huge parade is one of the biggest events of the year as massive balloons and floats make their way down 7th Ave.

December - Grand Central Laser Light Show A spectacular light show is beamed on to the ceiling on New York's central train station for 6 weeks at the end of every year.

Where to stay?

This is a personal preference and should be based on your interests and what attractions you plan to visit in the city. Midtown East (near Grand Central Terminal) is good for exploring the city. The best price/ performance ratio is East Williamsburg.

Long Island City is good if you want great **views of the Manhattan skyline** – just not too far to the east of Long Island, places like Montauk and the Hamptons are not budget.

Areas to avoid

DO NOT STAY OUTSIDE of the city. You will be reliant on the train schedule and round-trip tickets from to Grand Central were $20 per person during peak hours ($15 off-peak). When traveling with a group, the price of train tickets can add up and you will be better off using that money towards a room in the city.

The cheapest place to stay

If you're travelling solo hostels are your best option in New York, both for meeting people and saving pennies. Well-reviewed NY Moore Hostel is conveniently located in East Williamsburg and they offer dorms from $20.

We stayed in an Airbnb as we were two so it was cheaper - https://www.airbnb.com/rooms/30771254?s=51 and we took the transit bus in to the city. Airbnbs are expensive in New York but work out cheaper if you are travelling as a group.

Hack your New York Accommodation

Your two biggest expenses when travelling to New York are accommodation and food. This section is intended to help you cut these costs dramatically before and while you are in New York.

Hostels are the cheapest accommodation in New York but there are some creative workarounds to upgrade your stay on the cheap.

Use Time

There are two ways to use time. One is to book in advance. Three months will net you the best deal, especially if your visit coincides with an event. The other is to book on the day of your stay. This is a risky move, but if executed well, you can lay your head in a five-star hotel for a 2-star fee.

Before I travelled to New York, I checked for big events using a simple google search 'What's on in New York', there were no big events drawing travellers so I risked showing up with no accommodation booked (If there are big events on demand exceeds supply and you should avoid using this strategy) I started checking for discount rooms at 11 am using a private browser on booking.com.

Before I go into demand-based pricing, take a moment to think about your risk tolerance. By risk, I am not talking about personal safety. No amount of financial savings is worth risking that. What I am talking about is being inconvenienced. Do you deal well with last-minute changes? Can you roll with the punches or do you dislike it if something changes? Everyone is different and knowing yourself is the best way to plan a great trip. If you are someone that likes to have everything pre-planned using demand-based pricing to get cheap accommodation will not work for you. Skip this section and go to blind-booking.

Demand-based pricing

Be they an Airbnb host or hotel manager; no one wants empty rooms. Most will do anything to make some revenue because they still have the same costs to cover whether the room is occupied or not. That's why you will find many hotels drastically slashing room rates for same-day bookings.

How to book five-star hotels for a two-star price

You will not be able to find these discounts when the demand exceeds the supply. So if you're visiting during the peak season, or during an event which has drawn many travellers don't try this.

On the day of your stay, visit booking.com (which offers better discounts than Kayak and agoda.com). Hotel Tonight individually checks for any last-minute bookings, but they take a big chunk of the action, so the better deals come from booking.com. The best results come from booking between 2 pm and 4 pm when the risk of losing any revenue with no occupancy is most pronounced, so algorithms supporting hotels slash prices. This is when you can find rates that are not within the "lowest publicly visible" rate. To avoid losing customers to other websites, or cheapening the image of their hotel most will only offer the super cheap rates during a two hour window from 2 pm to 4 pm. Two guests will pay 10x difference in price but it's absolutely vital to the hotel that neither knows it.

Takeaway: To get the lowest price book on the day of stay between 2 pm and 4 pm and extend your search radius to include further afield hotels with good transport connections.

How to trick travel Algorithms to get the lowest hotel price

Do not believe anyone who says changing your IP address to get cheaper hotels or flights does NOT work. If you don't believe us, download a Tor Network and search for flights and hotels to one destination using your current IP and then the tor network (a tor browser hits your IP address from algorithms. It is commonly used by hackers). You will receive different prices.

The price you see is a decision made by an algorithm that adjusts prices using data points such as past bookings, remaining capacity, average demand and the probability of selling the room or flight later at a higher price. If booking. com knows you've searched for the area before it will keep the prices high. To circumvent this, you can either use a different IP address from a cafe or airport or data from an international sim. I use a sim from Three, which provides free data in many countries around the world. When you search from a new IP address, most of the time, and particularly near booking you will get a lower price. Sometimes if your sim comes from a 'rich' country, say the UK or USA, you will see higher rates as the algorithm has learnt people from these countries pay more. The solution is to book from a local wifi connection - but a different one from the one you originally searched from.

How to get last-minute discounts on owner rented properties

In addition to Airbnb, you can also find owner rented rooms and apartments on www.vrbo.com or HomeAway or a host of others. Nearly all owners renting accommodation will happily give renters a "last-minute" discount to avoid the space sitting empty, not earning a dime.

Go to Airbnb or another platform and put in today's date. Once you've found something you like start the negotiating by asking for a 25% reduction. A sample message to an Airbnb host might read:

Dear HOST NAME,

I love your apartment. It looks perfect for me. Unfortunately, I'm on a very tight budget. I hope you won't be offended, but I wanted to ask if you would be amenable to offering me a 25% discount for tonight, tomorrow and the following day? I see that you aren't booked. I can assure you, I will leave your place exactly the way I found it. I will put bed linen in the washer and ensure everything is clean for the next guest. I would be delighted to bring you a bottle of wine to thank you for any discount that you could offer.

If this sounds okay, please send me a custom offer, and I will book straight away.

YOUR NAME.

In my experience, a polite, genuine message like this, that proposes reciprocity will be successful 80% of the time. Don't ask for more than 25% off, this person still has to pay the bills and will probably say no as your stay will cost them more in bills than they make. Plus starting higher, can offend the owner and do you want to stay somewhere, where you have offended the host?

In Practice

To use either of these methods, you must travel light. Less stuff means greater mobility, everything is faster and you don't have to check-in or store luggage. If you have a lot of luggage, you're going to have fewer of these opportunities to save on accommodation. Plus travelling light benefits the planet - you're buying, consuming, and transporting less stuff.

Blind-booking

If your risk tolerance does not allow for last-minute booking, you can use blind-booking. Many hotels not wanting to cheapen their brand with known low-prices, choose to operate a blind booking policy. This is where you book without knowing the name of the hotel you're going to stay in until you've made the payment. This is also sometimes used as a marketing strategy where the hotel is seeking to recover from past issues. I've stayed in plenty of blind book hotels. As long as you choose 4 or 5 star hotels, you will find them to be clean, comfortable and safe. priceline.com, Hot Rate® Hotels and Top Secret Hotels (operated by lastminute.com) offer the best deals.

Hotels.com Loyalty Program

This is currently the best hotel loyalty program with hotels in New York. The basic premise is you collect 10 nights and get 1 free. hotels.com price match, so if booking.com has a cheaper price you can get hotel.com, to match. If you intend to travel more than ten nights in a year, its a great choice to get the 11th free.

Don't let time use you.

Rigidity will cost you money. You pay the price you're willing to pay, not the amount it requires a hotel to deliver. Therefore if you're in town for a big event, saving money on accommodation is nearly impossible so in such cases book three months ahead.

The best price performance location in New York

A room putting New York the local attractions, restaurants, and nightlife within walking distance will save you time on transport. However restaurants and bars don't get that much cheaper the further you go from famous tourist attractions. But you will also get a better idea of the day to day life of a local if you stay in a neighbourhood like East Williamsburg. It depends on the New York you want to experience. For the tourist experience stay in the centre either in a last-minute hotel or Airbnb. For a taste of local life the urban cool district of East Williamsburg is the best you will find. Studio Plus - Midtown Spacious Apartment is a luxurious apartment hotel in NoMad with consistent last minute rooms from $50 a night.

Saving money on New York Food

Breakfast

If you stay somewhere with a free breakfast, eat smart. Don't eat sugary cereals or white flour rich pastries if you don't want to be hungry an hour later. Before leaving your hotel or checking out, find some fresh fruit, water, and granola in the fitness centre or coffee in the lobby or business centre. If your hotel doesn't have free breakfast, don't take it. You can always eat cheaper outside. Johny's Luncheonette has the best cheap breakfast we found. Here you can pick up pancakes for less than $3.

Visit supermarkets at discount times.

You can get a 50 per cent discount around 5 pm at the Whole Foods supermarkets on fresh produce. The cheaper the supermarket, the less discounts you will find, so check Whole Foods supermarkets at 5 pm before the discount supermarkets. Some items are also marked down due to sell-by date after the lunchtime rush so its also worth to check in around 3 pm.

Use delivery services on the cheap.

Take advantage of local offers on food delivery services. Most platforms including Seamless and Door Dash offer $10 off the first order in New York.

SNAPSHOT: How to enjoy a $1,000 trip to New York for $200

(full breakdown at the end of the guide)

Stay	Private room - https://www.airbnb.com/rooms/5192219?s=51 $22
Eat	Average meal cost: $5 - $15
Move	Subway $32 for a weeks unlimited travel
See	Free museums, Staten Island Ferry, a Broadway show, markets, street art and so much more- $20
Total	US$200

Unique bargains I love in New York

New York has the reputation of being among the most luxurious and expensive destinations in the world. Fortunately, some of the best things in life are free (or almost free). There are a plethora of amazing free tours, free concerts, cheap theatre and film screenings, pay-what-you-wish nights at museums, city festivals, plus loads of green space to escape the urban sprawl.

Chelsea market and Gotham Food Hall are great for cheap eats. Also, it's always a good idea to picnic in Washington square park and Central Park (really any park). Murray's Cheese shop is near Washington square and you could get delicious grilled cheese or cheese/meat plate and bread and wine to take to the park - it makes for a lovely afternoon. Plus there are usually free shows in Bryant park and Central Park.

The first thing you should do when you arrive is check https://www.nycgo.com/maps-guides/free-in-nyc to see what free events are on. Many entice people to come with free food and drink.

How to use this book

Google and Tripadvisor are your on-the-go guides while travelling, a travel guide adds the most value during the planning phase, and if you're without wifi. Always download the google map for your destination - having an offline map will make using this guide much more comfortable. For ease of use, we've set the book out the way you travel starting with arriving, how to get around, then on to the money-saving tips. The tips we ordered according to when you need to know the tip to save money, so free tours and combination tickets feature first. We prioritised the rest of the tips by how much money you can save and then by how likely it was that you would be able to find the tip with a google search. Meaning those we think you could find alone are nearer the bottom. I hope you find this layout useful. If you have any ideas about making super cheap guides easy to use, please email me philgattang@gmail.-com .Now let's started with juicing the most pleasure from your trip to New York with the least possible money.

OUR SUPER CHEAP TIPS...

Arriving

There are three airports in New York and the cheapest way to and from them is with public transport.

From Newark: The trains from Newark costs $12.50 per person to Manhattan.

From LGA you can take M60 bus from all terminals at LaGuardia airport bus to 125th street in Manhattan for $2.75.

From JFK you'll have to take the airtrain to get on the subway system. Then the subway to your destination. One way $7.75.

Getting around

E-scooters/ bike sharing
Like a growing number of cities around the world, New York has a bike-sharing program - https://www.citibikenyc.com/pricing. A single ride is $3 or a day pass is $12.

Public transport
Get an unlimited MTA weekly card - $32 - to use the subway. It's the cheapest and easiest way to get around the city.

💡 INSIDER CULTURAL INSIGHT

As you sit on the subway imagine that one day be under the Ocean. As of 2019 2,500 decommissioned subway carriages have been sunk to provide habitats for sea creatures.

Get around for FREE
Use ride sharing service Lyft. Google for a free credit and open a new Lyft account. New York offers up to $50 free credit, which could cover your transport for your whole trip.

Walk – it's the best way to discover New York.

Start with a free walking tour

Forget exploring New York by wandering around aimlessly. Always start with a free organised tour if one is available. Nothing compares to local advice, especially when travelling on a budget. I gleamed many of our super cheap tips from local guides and locals in general, so start with a organised tour to get your bearings and ask for their recommendations for the best cheap eats, the best bargains, the best markets, the best place for a particular street eat. Perhaps some of it will be repeated from this guide, but it can't hurt to ask, especially if you have specific needs or questions. At the end you should leave an appropriate tip (usually around $5), but nobody bats an eye lid if you are unable or unwilling to do so, tell them you will leave a good review and always give them a little gift from home - I always carry small Vienna fridge magnets and I always tip the $5, but it is totally up to you.

The best free tour is with the greeters - locals who show you NYC. You can choose the neighborhood you want to tour, just book here: www.bigapplegreeter.org Reserve at least four weeks in advance to avoid disappointment.

There are 19 more free Tours available including Central Park. Lower Manhattan. 9/11 Memorial and World Trade Center. Greenwich Village. Food Tour of Greenwich Village. SoHo. The Brooklyn Bridge and The High Line: https://freetoursbyfoot.com/new-york-tours/

A note on paying for tours
The only time paying for a tour is worth it, is when you couldn't reach the place without the tour (e.g you need a boat), or when the tour is about the same price as the attraction entry. Otherwise you can do a range of self-guided tours using gpsmycity.com for FREE.

💡 INSIDER HISTORICAL INSIGHT

Standard street signs are green, look out for brown signs they mark historic districts.

💡 INSIDER MONEY SAVING TIP

Try Geocaching

This is where you hunt for hide-and-seek containers. You need a mobile device to follow the GPS clues in New York. A typical cache is a small, waterproof container with a logbook where you can leave a message or see various trinkets left by other cache hunters. Build your own treasure hunt by discovering geocaches in New York. www.geo-caching.com

New York Pass

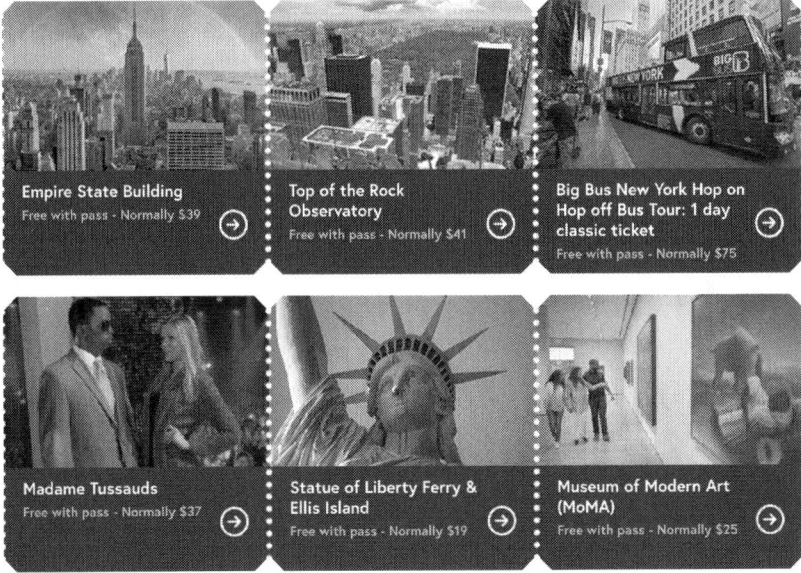

Empire State Building
Free with pass - Normally $39

Top of the Rock Observatory
Free with pass - Normally $41

Big Bus New York Hop on Hop off Bus Tour: 1 day classic ticket
Free with pass - Normally $75

Madame Tussauds
Free with pass - Normally $37

Statue of Liberty Ferry & Ellis Island
Free with pass - Normally $19

Museum of Modern Art (MoMA)
Free with pass - Normally $25

If you plan to hit all the major attractions in New York the New York pass can save you money on: Top of the Rock, Empire State Building, 9/11 Memorial Museum and 97 more attractions. Starting at $134 for adults for one day it is not cheap. However if you got up early to do the top attractions it works out at $19 per attraction. The key benefit is as well as saving money, you save time on queuing.

Buy the pass online and save 30% off the retail price. You can download the New York Pass mobile ticket. Consult the website to see if it matches your needs www.newyorkpass.com

Visit Free Museums

To make sure everybody has access to culture many of New York's top museums are free or have times when you can visit for free. Here are the best of the crop:

Always Free

National Museum of the American Indian
National September 11 Memorial
Museum at FIT - collection of garments & accessories
Hamilton Grange - preserves the relocated home of U.S. Founding Father Alexander Hamilton
American Folk Art Museum
Nicholas Roerich Museum Admission by Donation
American Museum of Natural History
Brooklyn Museum
Museum of the City of New York
Brooklyn Historical Society Free or Pay-What-You-Wish on Certain Days

Free at selected times

MoMA – 4–9pm Friday
MET - FREE every Friday from 4 pm-8 pm
Rubin Museum of Art – 6–10pm Friday
Asia Society & Museum – 6–9pm Friday, September to June
Japan Society – 6–9pm Friday
Frick Collection – 2–6pm Wednesday & 6–9pm first Friday of month
New Museum of Contemporary Art – 7–9pm Thursday
New-York Historical Society – 6–8pm Friday
Jewish Museum – 5–8pm Thursday and Saturday
Guggenheim Museum – 5:45–7:45pm Saturday
Whitney Museum of American Art – 7–10pm Friday
Neue Galerie – 6–8pm first Friday of month

Visit NYC's Top Free Historical Sights

• Ellis Island (New York Harbor)
• Gracie Mansion (Upper East Side)
• Merchant's House Museum (NoHo)
• Jane's Carousel (Brooklyn)
• Historic Richmond Town (Staten Island)

lk The High Line

The High Line is an elevated linear park, greenway and rail trail created on a former New York Central Railroad. It provides some of the best views of the city and is great for snapping photos. You start at Gansevoort Street in the Meatpacking District and end at West 34th Street, between 10th and 12th Avenues.

Visit two of New York's best known buildings

The first is the busy and bustling Grand Central Terminal at 46th St and Park Ave, while the other is the (understandably) far more subdued St Patrick's Cathedral on Fifth Avenue between 50th and 51st Sts.

Take the FREE Staten Island Ferry

The best way to see The Statue of Liberty is with the 25 minute FREE ride on the Staten Island ferry. Leaving from South Ferry Terminal in Lower Manhattan, on it you can enjoy breathtaking views of Lower Manhattan's skyline and an even better one of the Statue of Liberty. Be aware of scammers trying to sell tickets, the ferry is free.

From May to October, you can also take a FREE ferry over to Governors Island, a car-free island with great views.

For more adventure, take out a free kayak, available in the Hudson River Park, Brooklyn Bridge Park and Red Hook.

Cheap alternative to the Empire State Building

This famous art-deco skyscraper opened in 1930, it is no longer New York's tallest building but it has one of the best sunset views. Plus the newly added LED lights create more than 16 million color possibilities. If you go up to the top it will costs you $39. The best time to visit is sunset.

If you don't want to pay the $39 for the view head to Beekman Arms Hotel. The view from top is great. It is not the highest, but it is an intimate view and quite lovely. Plus, no one really goes there anymore so it's not touristy and it will cost you the price of a soda.

Walk across the Brooklyn Bridge

Jump on a 4, 5 or 6 train to Brooklyn Bridge. You will be at the Manhattan end of New York's most famous bridge. Afterwards take a break in the Empire Fulton Ferry State Park on the Brooklyn side.

Go to a top TV show for free

Fancy being in the audience of famous TV shows? Many are taped in New York City Including: The Late Show with Stephen Colbert, The Daily Show with Trevor Noah and The Tonight Show Starring Jimmy Fallon give free audience tickets out. Either go to TKTS booth in Times Square on Mondays or Tuesdays and you should find somebody heckling about free tickets or log on to www.nytix.com to reserve your spot.

Go to a Broadway show on the cheap

By buying your tickets on the day of the show you can get 50% cheaper. Either download the Today Tix app or go to the TKTS booth right in Times Square that opens twice a day and sells cheap broadway shows for that day. The big shows like Wicked and Book of Mormon won't have but you can find good seats for other major performances from $15.

If you're open to any show, try Broadway Roulette. You pick the day, it picks the show. You can get major productions from $49 - https://www.broadwayroulette.com/ I've been able to see so many awesome productions at great prices using this.

Visit New York Public Library

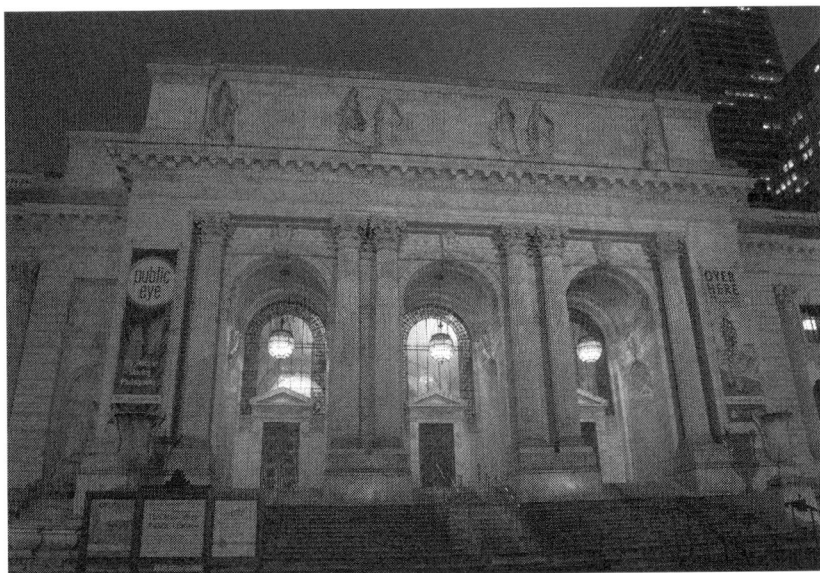

Built in 1911, it is the largest marble structure ever built in the United States. The New York Public Library is monumental and gorgeous inside. It is also an awesome place to go if you are looking for a quiet to escape NYC's crazy. My favourite place to read is the Rose Reading Room on the 3rd floor. There's also free wifi and charging sockets.

Go to the Bronx zoo for FREE!

Bronx Zoo is home to over 4,000 animals. Wednesday's are free at the Bronx Zoo, they do ask you to consider making a donation to help in caring for the 600 species of animals. This zoo emphasises the emotional connection and is a great way to spend a Wednesday afternoon. The food options are overprices, so bring your own snacks if you want them.

Watch free performances

Manhattan

SummerStage takes place from June through early September, and features over 100 free performances at 17 parks. Shakespeare in the Park, held also in Central Park. Top actors like Meryl Streep and Al Pacino have taken the stage in years past! Prospect Park has its own open-air summer concert and events series. Celebrate Brooklyn. https://www.bricartsmedia.org/events-performances/bric-celebrate-Brooklyn-festival

Free outdoor cinema

In summertime you can see free films at the River to River Festival (www.rivertorivernyc.com; at Hudson River Park in Manhattan and at Brooklyn Bridge Park www.brooklynbridgepark.org

Chck out the free HBO Bryant Park Summer Film Festival (www.bryantpark.org; hmid-Jun–Aug) screenings on Monday nights.

Free Live music

BAMcafe in Brooklyn has free concerts (world music, R&B, jazz, rock) on select Friday and Saturday nights. In Harlem, Marjorie Eliot opens her home for free jazz jams on Sunday.

Explore the markets

Chinatown.

Markets are a fun and eye-opening plunge into local culture and, unless you succumb to the persistent vendors, it will cost you nothing. Don't expect to find the bargain of a lifetime but Chinatown is always great browsing plus there are cheap dumplings, pork buns and hand-pulled noodles!

Brooklyn Flea. LIC Flea Market, Queens Night Market, Union Square Greenmarket. Chelsea Market, Red Hook Food Vendors (go if you love Latin American food) are all worth checking out.

Stiles Farmers Market is a Neighbourhood grocer offering a wide variety of fresh produce & baked goods at discount prices.

Century 21, have designer goods for cheap - gets very crowded on Saturdays and Sundays.

Go to an auction

Christie's New York is always free to visit. They have guest lectures, a beautiful gallery with diverse exhibits all for FREE!

Address: Rockefeller Center

Watch Free comedy

There are over 230 free comedy shows a month throughout NYC, Brooklyn, and Queens! Here are the best of the crop:

- The Lantern Comedy Club
- "Hot Soup" at Irish Exit. Midtown East. Tuesdays at 8pm.
- "Gandhi, Is That You" at Lucky Jack's. LES. Wednesdays at 9pm.
- "Whiplash" at Upright Citizens Brigade. Chelsea. Mondays at 11pm.
- "Broken Comedy" at Bar Matchless. Greenpoint.
- Open mic night at Legion Bar. Williamsburg.

Chill out in Central Park

Affectionately known as 'The Lungs of New York', Central Park is one of the most beautiful parts of New York and you can see why locals love it so much. Stretching from 59th St in Midtown Manhattan to 110th St in Harlem its a refuge from the cities chaos. It has free wifi, so you can still stay on, if you want to.

⚲ INSIDER MONEY SAVING TIP

If central Park is overcrowded head to Governors Island its home to a 25-foot hill that offers a 360-degree view of the city's harbour.

Church Hop

Not only exceptional architecturally and historically, New York's churches contain exquisite art, artefacts and other priceless treasures. Best of all, entry to general areas within them is, in most cases, free. Do respect the fact that although many of the places of worship are also major tourist attractions. Trinity Church Wall Street, St. Patrick's Cathedral (already mentioned) Grace Church, Hillsong Church Manhattan, The Brooklyn Tabernacle are the best of the crop.

Thrift shop

Thrift stores in NYC are some of the best in the world, but theres stiff competition for the best bargains. Go early and bring snacks for energy to hunt down designer pieces. Here are the best thrift stores: Lot Less Closeouts. 206 W 40th St, Artists and Fleas at Chelsea Market. 88 Tenth Ave, 15th Street (btwn W 15th & 16th St), Chelsea. Philip Williams Posters. 122 Chambers St and Housing Works Thrift Shop. What you want to look for are the ones located in affluent areas with low-income foot-fall. If you're not familiar with the area and asking around hasn't returned any results, here's what you can do. Google for the most expensive area to live in NYC, sometimes they are a little outside the city. Then put the American term Thrift store into Google Maps. Start with the most expensive and work your way through until the middle-tier ones. You will be surprised what you find.

Hunt for rare first editions

Pay a visit to Westsider Rare & used Books store offering fiction, art books, children's literature & rock music albums. You never know what you will uncover.

Explore NYC Street art

Here are the best Places To spot Colorful murals and graffiti art in NYC:

Streets:
• Broadway & W. 79th St.
• Madison Ave.
• Second Avenue and First Street.
• East Village.

Galleries
• Centre-fuge **Public Art** Project's rotating gallery.
• Lower East Side's Freeman Alley.
• Graffiti Hall of Fame's Latin American art.
• 'Love Vandal' by Nick Walker's

- Welling Court Mural Project, Queens' premier street-art gallery.

Food and drink tips

Amazing falafel sandwich for $5

Oasis in Williamsburg (right outside the Bedford avenue stop) do amazing falafel sandwich for $5 or chicken kebab for $6. Also the green taco truck on Bedford Avenue (parked outside the Starbucks) has the best burrito I've had in New York for $8 (get the steak one).

Best bagel place

The best bagel in the city comes from Ess-A-Bagel in midtown east. $5 but absolutely amazing!

Best bang for your buck all-you-can-eat

A B Sushi Japanese is an all you can eat buffet that will blow your mind. I cannot believe a place like this exists in New York. Delicious sushi is a given in NYC, however delicious sushi and being reasonably priced is a rare occurrence. Go for lunch and pay $18 for all you can eat sushi. All you can eat buffets are a great way to stock on on nutritious food while travelling. Dishes like fish are normally expensive, but here you can chow down on your omega 3's for much less. Don't drink much water or eat tons of rice and you'll get more than your money's worth.
Address: W 36th St

Eat dinner during happy hour

New York restaurants are pricey, look for happy hours, they can be a great way to save money - 4:00pm and goes until 8:00pm (or closing). Food specials can include pre-fix menus, 50% off starters, $1 oysters or 20% off the food menu depending on the restaurant.

Find deals to eat out

Great sites to visit include Yelp Deals, Groupon, LivingSocial, and Valpak. You can also find coupons at places such as your local hotel, bus or train stations, and the airport, so keep your eyes open.

Free coffee refill

If you need a laptop day head to Thrillist an ever growing New York City coffee chain, which serves Seattle's Caffe refills on iced coffee and filter coffees.

Free Food

And if you're really hard up you can go to The New York City ISKCON Temple for free food iskconnyc.com For ethical reasons I would only go here, if you're really struggling, and if you are, firstly, I'm sorry, that sucks. Make sure to check out our section on finding work while travelling. Things like teaching English online are easy to get started.

Nightlife – Bars & Clubs

If you don't go out you'll miss out on some great venues – the clubs and bars make it hard to catch some sleep in New York but prices for indulging nocturnal desires aren't cheap. Here are some places to drink on the cheap - beers under $4!

- Johnny's Bar
- Rudy's Bar & Grill
- Local 138
- Jimmy's Corner
- Barcelona bar in Hell's Kitchen - Kind of a dive but so entertaining & they have very cheap drinks for Manhattan.

- Botanica Bar The place is a bit on the dark side, but the prices and happy hour make braving it worth-while.

Don't leave New York without seeing

Statue of Liberty
Iconic National Monument opened in 1886, offering guided tours, a museum & city views.

Times Square
Bustling destination in the heart of the Theater District known for bright lights, shopping & shows.

Metropolitan Museum of Art
A grand setting for one of the world's greatest collections of art, from ancient to contemporary.

Brooklyn Bridge
Beloved, circa-1883 landmark connecting Manhattan & Brooklyn via a unique stone-&-steel design.

Rockefeller Center
Famous complex that's home to TV studios, plus a seasonal ice rink & giant Christmas tree.

Grand Central Terminal
Iconic train station known for its grand facade & main concourse, also offering shops & dining.

The Battery
Historic park with Ellis Island & Statue of Liberty views & ferry service to both islands.

Theatre District
The Theater District is the teeming heart of Midtown West. In the pedestrian plazas of Times Square, costumed characters beckon to energetic crowds.

Liberty Island
Audio & guided tours are offered on this iconic island featuring the Statue of Liberty & a museum.

9/11 Memorial
Plaza, pools & exhibits honoring victims of 1993 & 2001 WTC terrorist attacks. Free timed admission.

SoHo, Manhattan
Designer boutiques, fancy chain stores and high-end art galleries make trendy SoHo a top shopping destination, especially for out-of-towners. Known for its elegant cast-iron-facades and cobblestones.

Coney Island
Coney Island morphs into an entertainment destination each summer with its theme park.

American Museum of Natural History
From dinosaurs to outer space and everything in between, this huge museum showcases natural wonders.

Solomon R. Guggenheim Museum
Frank Lloyd Wright–designed modern-art museum with an architecturally significant spiral rotunda.

The Plaza
Iconic 19th-century lodging offering fine dining & afternoon tea, plus a champagne bar & a spa.

Greenwich Village
The epicenter of the city's 1960s counterculture movement, the tree-lined streets of Greenwich Village are now a hub of Jazz clubs and Off-Broadway Theaters.

Bryant Park

Green space behind the NY Public Library's main branch, with 4 acres, a cafe and other food kiosks.

Flatiron Building
Architect Daniel Burnham's iconic 1902 triangular tower nicknamed for its clothes iron look.

DUMBO
Trendy Dumbo's cobblestone streets and converted Brooklyn warehouse buildings are the backdrop for independent boutiques, high-end restaurants and trendy cafes.

Little Italy
Little Italy welcomes a heavily tourist crowd to its high concentration of souvenir shops and traditional Italian eateries and bakeries.

Union Square
The lively Union Square neighborhood is anchored by it's namesake pedestrian plaza and bustling park, which attracts a mix of professionals, street artists, students and protesters.

Lower East Side
The eclectic Lower East Side is where gritty alleys and tenement-style buildings mix with upscale apartments and chic boutiques. Nighttime draws hip, young crowds.

Washington Square Park
Historic Greenwich Village concrete-&-green park known for its stately arch & prime people-watching.

Financial District
This is the city's buzzing financial heart, home to Wall Street and glittering skyscrapers. Sidewalks bustle during the week and, after work, young professionals fill the restaurants and bars.

Intrepid Sea, Air & Space Museum
Flight museum on an aircraft carrier whose exhibits include a Concorde, submarine & space shuttle.

Meatpacking District
The Meatpacking District is a hip commercial area on the far west side. It's home to the Whitney Museum of American Art and high-end designer clothing stores.

Manhattan Bridge
Opened in 1909, this suspension bridge between Brooklyn & Manhattan.

Is the tap water drinkable?

Yes.

Haggle-o-meter

How much can you save haggling here?

Gentle haggling is common at markets in NYC. Haggling in stores is generally unacceptable, although some good-humoured bargaining at smaller artisan or craft shops is cool if you are making multiple purchases.

Enjoy your first Day for under $20

Start early by visiting the American Museum of Natural History for free. Then great a cheap bagel and coffee and take a couple of hours to explore Central Park. Enjoy highlights such as Strawberry Fields, Sheeps Meadow, the Bow Bridge and the Bethesda Fountain. Follow the aromas to one of the numerous delis on 7th Ave. Explore Midtown Manhattan, visiting Times Square, Fifth Avenue, the Madison Square Garden and much more. Take the 1 train from Times Square to South Ferry. Jump on board the Staten Island ferry for unforgettable views of the Statue of Liberty. Take the 1 train back up to Christopher St/Sheridan Square. Get take away pizza in 'Bleecker St Pizza' both in the West Village. Wander down Bleecker Street until you come to MacDougal St - the heart of Greenwich Village. Go for a beer in one of the many bars before heading home to sleep.

Websites to save you Money

1. **TalkTalkbnb.com** - Here you stay for free when you teach the host your native language
2. Rome2Rio.com - the go to site for good travel prices on train, bus, planes etc. Especially good for paths less travelled.
3. couchsurfing.com - stay for free with a local - always check reviews.
4. trustedhousesitter.com - always check reviews
5. booking.com - now sends you vouchers for discounts in the city when you book through them
6. blablacar.com - travel in car with locals already going to your destination
7. airbnb.com for both accommodation and experiences.
8. hostelbookers.com - book hostels
9. https://freetoursbyfoot.com/new-york-tours - free walking tours
10. https://www.groupon.com/local/new-york - deals
11. https://www.timeout.com/newyork/shopping/top-ten-free-new-york-city-discount-shopping-apps - shopping deals
12. https://www.citypass.com/new-york - good if you plan to see most attractions. Bad if you visit only a handful.
13. https://www.nycgo.com/maps-guides/free-in-nyc - free events

Need to Know

Currency: Dollar

Language: English

Money: Widely available ATMs.

Visas: The US Visa Waiver Program allows nationals of 38 countries to enter the US without a visa, but
you must fill out an ESTA application before departing.
http://www.doyouneedvisa.com/

Time: GMT - 5

When to Go

High Season: July and August.

Shoulder: May, April, June

Low Season: September to May.

Important Numbers

113 Ambulance

112 Police

Watch to understand the History

New York 's history is fascinating. There are tons of documentaries. This is great and takes you to 1825 - https://www.youtube.com/watch?v=yumVGUA1Fcl

Cheapest route to NYC from Europe

At the time of writing Norwegian are flying to New York for around $260 return from Paris to NYC. I specialise in finding cheap flights, so if you need help finding a cheap flight simply review this book and send me an email.
philgtang@gmail.com

From	To	Depart	Return
France (Any)	New York, NY (Any)	Cheapest mo...	Cheapest mo...

☐ Direct flights only

Estimated lowest prices only. Found in the last 15 days.

Select departure city

Lyon
1+ stops   from **$265** 〉

Paris
Direct   from **$284** 〉

Nice
1+ stops (Direct available)   from **$315** 〉

Châlons-en-Champagne
1+ stops   from **$343** 〉

Must-try New York Street Foods

New York has so many good restaurants. But there are also dishes that are best enjoyed on the streets. Here are the ones you must-try:

- Bagels
- Pizza
- Falafel
- Taco's and Burritos
- Pastrami sandwiches
- Baked pretzels.
- New York cheesecake.

You will find at least five of these being sold from a street food vendor on every corner.

Cheap Eats

If you tire of eating street foods go to these sit-down restaurants to fill your stomach without emptying your wallet by trying these local restaurants with mains under $8.

(Download the offline map on google maps, (instructions 1. go to app 2. select offline apps in the left sidebar 3. go to the area you want to download 4. click download). Then simply type the restaurant names in to navigate, star them so you can see where the cheap eats are when you're out and about to avoid wasting your money at hyped tourist joints)

Los Tacos
Bustling taqueria serving tacos, quesadillas & aguas frescas in a street-style set-up (no seating).

Vanessa's Dumpling House
Steamed-while-you-wait dumplings & other Chinese fare served in basic surrounds.

88 Lan Zhou Handmade Noodles
Bare-bones Chinese noodle joint slinging classic, house-made-dough dishes (no alcohol & cash only).

Cheeky Sandwiches
A hip sandwich shop offering a select menu of po' boys & other Big Easy bites in a tiny storefront.

Taqueria Diana
This small, utilitarian Mexican restaurant serves tacos, burritos, nachos, roast chicken & more.

Baohaus

Savory Taiwanese steamed buns are the specialty of this bare-bones East Village eatery.

Margon
Small Latin counter-service spot serving Cuban sandwiches, American breakfasts & salads.

goa taco
Cozy counter-service joint offering creative, globally-inspired tacos in paratha shells.

Manousheh
Brick-walled eatery specializing in savory & sweet Lebanese flatbreads baked in-house.

Blue Collar
Counter-serve burger joint serving griddled burgers, fries & handmade shakes in a retro space.

Thelewala
Bustling spot that's open late turning out classic Indian street eats in a compact, mod storefront.

Papaya King
Counter-service eatery serving budget-friendly hot dogs & papaya drinks in a no-frills setting.

Sons of Thunder
Customizable poké bowls plus burgers & shakes in counter-serve digs with a big, airy seating area.

ilili Box
Inventive Lebanese bites are served at this food-stand offshoot of a local, upscale restaurant.

Egg Shop
Sunny little cafe focusing on everything egg including creative sandwiches, fancy Benedicts & more.

Comfort food · Breakfast · Small plates

Mimi Cheng's Dumplings
Several different Chinese dumplings made from family recipes star at this tiny spot with few seats.

Mamoun's Falafel
Longtime local Middle Eastern chain serving falafel, shawarma, kebabs & more in a traditional space.
The falafels are always filling , cheap and the white sauce will dance on your tongue.

Little Saigon Pearl
Good food and cheap! Definitely my favorite Vietnamese in New York.

Avoid these tourist traps or scams

Scams and trickery are the scourge of a traveler's budget and unfortunately scams abound in NYC, and particularly near the attractions. If someone approaches you and you fear their intentions just say 'sorry, no english.' and walk on.

A well known scam is scammers selling fake tickets to get onto Liberty island, the island holding the Statue of Liberty. Only one company, Statue Cruises, sells these tickets, buy them online to avoid being conned by official looking salesmen - there are tons of conman there and they look legit.

It's not a scam but don't get on the local subway trains, they will take twice the time. Also don't stop in the middle of the sidewalk to take pictures - locals will shout at you.

Getting Out

Bus

Megabus
Booking ahead can save you up to 98% of the cost of the ticket. Check megabus.com for destinations from NYC.

Plane

At the time of writing Spirit are offering the cheapest flights onwards.Take advantage of discounts and specials. Sign up for e-newsletters from local carriers including Spirit to learn about special fares. Be careful with cheap airlines, most will allow hand-luggage only, and some charge for anything that is not a backpack. Check their websites before booking if you need to take luggage.

From	To	Depart	Return
NYC, NY (Any)	Everywhere	Cheapest mo...	[One Way]

Direct flights only

Estimated lowest prices only. Found in the last 15 days.

United States	from $41	⌄
Canada	from $57	⌄
Guadeloupe	from $58	⌄
Martinique	from $58	⌄
Guatemala	from $81	⌄
Mexico	from $82	⌄

FREE BOOK

GET ANY 2020 SUPER CHEAP GUIDE FREE

REVIEW THIS GUIDE TO RECEIVE THE 2020 EDITION OF ANY SUPER CHEAP GUIDE **FREE**. Go to

with a screenshot of your review to claim YOUR FREE book.

Personal Cost Breakdown

	How	Cost normally / advice	Cost when following suggested tip
How I got from the airport to the city	$2.75 subway	$50 Taxi	$2.75
Where I stayed	airbnb in the city - https://www.airbnb.com/rooms/21727317?s=51 $22	Hotels are upwards of $150 a night.	$66
Tastiest street foods I ate and cost	Bagel's, pizza, sushi	You can eat well in NYC without spending a lot.	$5 - $15 per meal
How I got around	subway unlimited week card	The subway is fast and reliable. Avoid travelling 4 - 7pm - rush hour is real.	$32
What I saw and paid	20ish free museums, parks, buildings, churches, Broadway show	You don't need to spend a lot to have an amazing adventure in NYC.	$20 on the broadway show
My onward flight	Orlando	Book six weeks ahead for the lowest prices	$40
My Total costs	US$200		$200

The secret to saving HUGE amounts of money when travelling to New York is...

Your mindset. Money is an emotional topic, if you associate words like cheapskate, Miser (and its £9.50 to go into Charles Dickens London house, oh the Irony) with being thrifty when travelling you are likely to say 'F-it' and spend your money needlessly because you associate pain with saving money. You pay now for an immediate reward. Our brains are prehistoric; they focus on surviving day to day. Travel companies and hotels know this and put trillions into making you believe you will be happier when you spend on their products or services. Our poor brains are up against outdated programming and an onslaught of advertisements bombarding us with the message: spending money on travel equals PLEASURE. To correct this carefully lodged propaganda in your frontal cortex you need to imagine your future self.

Saving money does not make you a cheapskate. It makes you smart. How do people get rich? They invest their money. They don't go out and earn it; they let their money earn more money. So every time you want to spend money, imagine this: while you travel your money is working for you, not you for money. While you sleep the money you've invested is going up and up. That's a pleasure a pricey entrance fee can't give you. Thinking about putting your money to work for you tricks your brain into believing you are not withholding pleasure from yourself, you are saving your money to invest so you can go to even more amazing places. You are thus turning thrifty travel into a pleasure fueled sport.

When you've got money invested - If you want to splash your cash on a first-class airplane seat - you can. I can't tell you how to invest your money, only that you should. Saving $20 on taxi's doesn't seem like much but over time you could be saving upwards of $15,000 a year, which is a deposit for a house which you can rent on Airbnb to finance more travel. Your brain making money looks like your brain on cocaine, so tell yourself saving money is making money.

Scientists have proved that imagining your future self is the easiest way to associate pleasure with saving money. You can download FaceApp — which will give you a picture of what you will look like older and greyer, or you can take a deep breath just before spending money and ask yourself if you will regret the purchase later.

The easiest ways to waste money travelling are:

Getting a taxi. The solution to this is to always download the google map before you go. Many taxi drivers will drive you around for 15 minutes when the place you were trying to get to is a 5-minute walk… remember while not getting an overpriced taxi to tell yourself, 'I am saving money to free myself for more travel.'
Spending money on overpriced food when hungry. The solution: carry snacks. A banana and an apple will cost you, in most places less than a dollar.
Spending on entrance fees to top-rated attractions. If you really want to do it, spend the money happily. If you're conflicted sleep on it. I don't regret spending $200 on a skydive over the Great Barrier Reef, I do regret going to the top of the shard in London for $60. Only you can know but make sure it's your decision and not the marketing directors at said top-rated attraction.
Telling yourself 'you only have the chance to see/eat/experience it now'. While this might be true, make sure YOU WANT to spend the money. Money spent is money you can't invest, and often you can have the same experience for much less.

You can experience luxurious travel on a small budget which will trick your brain into thinking you're already a high-roller, which will mean you'll be more likely to start acting like one and invest your money. Stay in five-star hotels for $5 by booking on the day of your stay on booking.com to enjoy last minute deals. You can go to fancy restaurants using daily deal sites. Ask your airline about last minute upgrades to first-class or business. I paid $100 extra on a $179 ticket to Cuba from Germany to be bumped to Business Class. When you ask you will be surprised what you can get both at hotels and airlines.

Travel, as the saying goes is the only thing you spend money on that makes you richer. In practice, you can easily waste money, making it difficult to enjoy that metaphysical wealth. The biggest money saving secret is to turn bargain hunting into a pleasurable activity, not an annoyance. Budgeting consciously can be fun, don't feel disappointed because you don't spend the $60 to go into an attraction, feel good because soon that $60 will soon be earning money for you. Meaning, you'll have the time and money to enjoy more metaphysical wealth, while your bank balance increases.

So there it is, you can save a small fortune by being strategic with your trip planning. We've arranged everything in the guide to offer the best bang for your buck. Which means we took the view that if it's not a good investment for your money, we wouldn't include it. Why would a guide called 'Super Cheap' include lots of overpriced attractions? That said if you think we've missed something or have unanswered questions ping me an email philgtang@gmail.com I'm on central Europe time and usually reply within 8 hours of getting your mail.

Don't put your dreams off!

Time is a currency you never get back and travel is its greatest return on investment. Plus now you know you can visit New York for a fraction of the price most would have you believe. Go and have a fantastic time!

Thank you for reading

Dear Lovely Reader,

If you have found this book useful, please consider writing a short review on Amazon.

One person from every 1000 readers leaves a review on Amazon. It would mean more than you could ever know if you were one of our 1 in 1000 people to take the time to write a short review.

We are a group of four friends who all met travelling 15 years ago. We believe that great experiences don't need to blow your budget, just your mind.

Thank you so much for reading again and for spending your time and investing your trips future in Super Cheap Guides Guides.

Phil

P.S If you need any more super cheap tips we'd love to hear from you e-mail me at philgtang@gmail.com, we have a lot of contacts in every region, so if there's a specific bargain you're hunting we can help you find it :-)

GET 300 TRAVEL GUIDES FULL OF SUPER CHEAP TIPS FREE ON AMAZON WITH KINDLE UNLIMITED.

UNCOVERED A SUPER CHEAP TIP DURING YOUR TRAVELS? GET PAID FOR IT. EMAIL PHILGTANG@GMAIL.COM

WE PAY FOR TIPS

CHOOSE FROM PRO RATA ROYALTIES OR A $50 AMAZON VOUCHER

Bonus Budget Travel Hacks

I've included these bonus travel hacks to help you plan and enjoy the trip cheaply, joyfully and smoothly.

How NOT to be ripped off

The thrill of spontaneity is incredible, but if you do a little planning ahead, you will not only save yourself from several mental troubles, but also a lot of money. I am the laziest of planners when it comes to travelling, but I make sure I begin a trip well.

1. **Never ever agree to pay as much as you want trap. Always decide on a price before.**

Whoever you're dealing with is trained to tell you, they are uninterested in money! This is a trap. If you let people do this they will ask for MUCH MORE money at the end, and because you have used there service, you will feel obliged to pay. This is a conman's trick and nothing more.

2. Choose to stay in a hostel, instead of a hotel the first nights to get the lay of the land.

get a chance to learn so much. I have also observed that the location of hostels is often close to main attractions. Also please do not worry about luxury, you are going to spend most of your time outside anyway.

3. Pack light

You can move faster and easier. If you take heavy luggage so you will end up taking cabs which are comparatively very costly.

4. If a local approaches you, they are normally trying to scam you, this is ALWAYS true in tourist destinations.

5. Don't book for more than two days and note down the address on your phone

Unless the place you're doing is going to be busy. e.g Alaska in summer.

6. Withdraw cash from ATM's when you need it, don't carry it with you.

5. NEVER use the airport taxi service. Plan to use public transport before you reach the airport

6. Don't buy a sim card from the airport, but from the local supermarkets it will be 50% less.

7. Eat at local restaurants serving regional food
Food defines culture. Exploring all delights available to the palate.

How to overcome travel related struggles

Anxiety when flying

It has been over 40 years since a plane has been brought down because of turbulence. 40 years! Planes are built to withstand lighting strikes, extreme storms and ultimately can adjust course to get out of their way. Landing and take over are when the most accidents happen, but you have statistically three times the chance of winning a huge jackpot lottery, then you do of crashing then.

If you feel afraid on the flight focus on your breathing saying the word 'smooth' over and over until the flight is smooth. Always check the airline safety record airlinerating.com I was surprised to learn Ryanair and Easyjet as much less safe than Wizz Air according to those ratings. If there is extreme turbulence, I feel much better knowing I'm in a 7 star safety plane.

Wanting to sleep instead of seeing new places

This is a common problem. Just relax, there's little point doing fun things when you feel tired. Plan and fact in jetlag.

Going over budget

Come back from a trip to a monster credit card bill? You're not alone. These are the costs that can crept up. Don't let them.

- To and from the airport. Solution: leave adequate time and take the cheapest method - book before.
- Baggage. Solution: take hand luggage and post things you might need to yourself.
- Eating out. Solution: go to cheap eats places and suggest those to friends.
- Parking. Solution: use apps to find free parking
- Tipping. Solution Leave a modest tip and tell the server you will write them a nice review.
- Souvenirs. Solution: fridge magnets only.
- Giving to the poor. (This one still gets me, but if you're giving away $10 a day - it adds up) Solution: volunteer your time at a local soup kitchens.

Price v Comfort

I love traveling, I don't love struggling. I like decent accommodation, being able to eat properly and see places and enjoy. I am never in the mood for low cost airlines or crappy transfers so here's what I do to save money.

- Avoid organised tours unless you are going to a place where safety is a real issue. They are expensive and constrain your wanderlust to typical things. Note, I only recommend them in Algeria, Iran and Papua New Guinea - where language and gender views pose serious problems all cured by a reputable tour organiser.
- Eat what the locals do.
- Cook in your airbnb/ hostel where restaurants are expensive.
- Shop at local markets.
- Never take the first price.

- Spend time choosing your flight, and check the operator on ari-lineratings.com
- Mix up hostels and Airbnbs. Hostels for meeting people, Airbnb for relaxing and feeling 'at home'.

Not knowing where toilets are

Use Toilet Finder - https://play.google.com/store/apps/details?id=com.bto.toilet&hl=en

Your airbnb is awful

Airbnb customer service is notoriously bad. Help yourself out. Never book somewhere without at least 5 reviews. Try to sort things out with the host, but if you can't take photos of everything e.g bed, bathroom, mess, doors, contact them within 24 hours and tell them you had to leave and pay for new accommodation. And ask politely for a full refund.

The airline loses your bag

Take a photo of your checked luggage before you check it.
Go to the Luggage desk before leaving the airport and report the bag missing.
Most airlines will give you an overnight bag, ask where your staying and return the bag to you within three days. Its extremely rare for them to completely lose it these days, but if that happens you should submit an insurance claim.

Your travel companion lets you down.

Whether it's a breakup or a friend cancelling, it sucks and can ramp up costs. In these cases, I normally go to a well-reviewed hostel and find someone I want to travel with - if I need someone to cover the extra costs.

Culture shock

I had one of the strongest culture shocks while spending 6 months in Japan. It was overwhelming how much I actually had to prepare when I went outside of the door (googling words and sentences what to use, where to go, which station and train line to use, what is this food called in Japanese and how does its look etc.). I was so tired constantly but in the end I just let go and went with my extremely bad Japanese. I was trying to ask for soup one day and asked for help with my piles… the people were laughing so hard one actually choked.

If you feel culture shocked its because your brain is referencing your surroundings to what you know. My tip is to just let go and learn some of the local language. You won't like everywhere you go - but you can at least relax everywhere you go.

You're tired

I feel like I just want to go go go go go and See everything and don't let myself just take some time to rest without feeling guilty or conflicted but its important to rest when travelling. I like to create a mini entertainment zone, and occasionally binge watch something or watch documentaries about where I currently am on YouTube.

Car rental

I always use carrentals.com and book with a credit card. Most credit cards will give you free insurance for the car, so you don't need to pay the extra.

You're sick

First off ALWAYS, purchase travel insurance. Including emergency transport up to $500k even to back home, which is usually less than $10 additional. I use https://www.comparethemarket.com/travel-insurance/

If I am sick I normally check into a hotel with room service and ride it out.

Make a Medication Travel Kit

Take medications with you, it is always more expensive to buy there unless you are lucky.

- Antidiarrheal medication (for example, bismuth subsalicylate, loperamide)
- Antihistamine.
- Anti-motion sickness medication.
- Medicine for pain or fever (such as acetaminophen, aspirin, or ibuprofen)
- Mild laxative.
- Cough suppressant/expectorant.
- Throat Lozenges

Save yourself from most travel related hassle

- Do not screw around with immigration and customs staff. You will lose.

- Book the most direct flight you can find, nonstop if possible. Keep weather in mind with connecting flights and watch out for connections in cities with multiple airports through different airports (airlines sometimes connect this way... watch it in places like London and New York)

- Carry a US$ 100 bill for emergency cash. I have entered a country and all ATM and credit card systems were down. US$ can be exchanged nearly anywhere in the world.

- Pack light. Pack light. Pack light. Pack light.

- On long connections, many airport lounges are pay lounges and can be very comfortable and cheaper than a transit hotel.

- Check, and recheck, required visas and such BEFORE the day of your trip. Some countries, for instance, require a ticket out of the country in order to enter. Others, like the US and Australia, require electronic authorization in advance.

- McDonalds and Starbucks offer free wifi in most of the world.

- Security is asinine and inconsistent around the world. Keep this in mind when connecting flights. Always leave at least 2 hours for international connections or international to domestic.

- Expats are rarely the best source for local information. Lots of barstool pontificates in the world.

- Wiki travel is perfect to use for a lay of the land

- Expensive luggage rarely lasts longer than cheap luggage, in my experience. Fancy leather bags are usually toast with air travel.

- Buy travel insurance. A comprehensive annual policy is best and not that expensive.

- Learning to say please and thank you in the local language is not that hard and opens doors. As does a smile and a handshake.

Where and How to Make Friends

Become popular at the airport

Want to become popular at the airport? Pack a power bar with multiple outlets and just see how many friends you make. It's amazing how many people forget their chargers, or who packed them in the luggage that they checked in!

Stay in Hostels

I note there's a line about backpacking, young, confident, hostel demographic that seems to have a whole unspoken backstory going on.

First of all, Hostels don't have to be shared dorms, and they cater to a much wider demographic than is assumed in the OP's comments. In my experience hostels were a way better environment for meeting people than hotels, and more importantly they tended to open up excursion opportunities that further opened up that opportunity. Hotel guests tend to be more cocooned, either couples or families, or if solo, more often than not business travellers, who are rarely interested in chit-chat.

Or take up a hobby

However, if hostels are a definite no-no; find an interest. Take up a hobby where you will meet people. I've dived for years and the nature of diving is you're always paired up with a dive buddy, and I met a lot of interesting people that way. Find something like that the gets people together. However, all of this is about creating the opportunity, you still have to take it, and if you're not the most outgoing person, pack the power supply.

GENERAL HACKS

From saving space in your suitcase to scoring cheap flights, there are a wealth of travel hacks that can help you use to have a stress-free and happy travels without breaking the bank.

Planning and booking stages of travel are equally instrumental in how successful your trip will be, which can be a lot of pressure.

Before You Go

Money

- Get cash from ATMs for best rates.
- Never change at airport exchange desks unless you absolutely have to, then just change enough to get to an ATM.
- Charles Schwab High Yield Checking accounts refund every single ATM fee worldwide, require no minimum balance and have no monthly fee.
- Bring a spare credit card for real emergencies.
- Split cash in various places on your person (pockets, shoes) and in your luggage.
- Use a money belt under your clothes or put $50 in your shoe/ bra incase.

Food

-
- When it comes to food, eat in local restaurants, not tourist-geared joints or choose a hostel.
- with facilities and cook for yourself. The same goes for drinking and going out.

- Bring boiled eggs, canned tuna and nuts with you to avoid being caught out by extreme hunger and having to buy expensive/ unhealthy foods full of sugar.
- Take a spork - a knife, spoon and fork all in one.

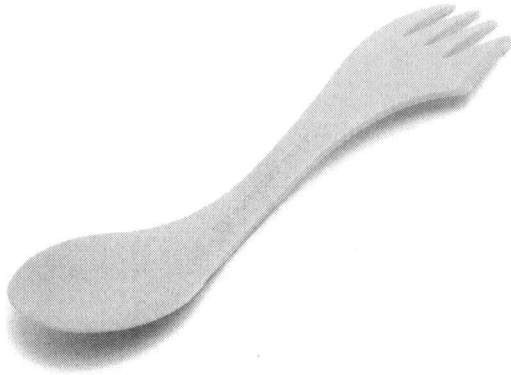

Water Bottle

Take a water bottle with a filter. We love these ones from Water to Go.
Empty it before airport security and seperate the two pieces.

Bug Sprays

Always buy on Amazon. If you have an urgent need while travelling you will pay over the odds. If you are especially tasty to mosquitoes spray your clothes with Permethrin before you travel. A 'Bite Away' zapper can be used after the bite to totally erase it. It cuts down on the itching and need for anti-hestimaines

Order free mini's

Don't buy those expensive travel sized toiletries, order travel sized freebies online. This gives you the opportunity to try brands you've never used before, and who knows, you might even find your new favourite soap.

CHEAP FLIGHT HACKS

Use skyscanner.net - they include the low-cost airlines that others like Kayak leave out.

Use open parameters, e.g if you want to fly from Chicago to Paris, put in USA to France, you may find flights from NYC to Paris for $70 and can take a cheap flight to NYC. Calculate full costs, including accommodation and getting to and from airports before bookting.

ALWAYS USE A PRIVATE BROWSER TO BOOK FLIGHTS

Skyscanner and other sites track your IP address and put prices up and down based on what they determine your desire to buy. e.g if you've booked one-way and are looking for the return these sites will jack the prices up by in most cases 50%. Incognito browsing pays.

Use a VPN such as Hola to book your flight from your destination

Install Hola, change your destination, the location from which a ticket is booked can affect the price. Try using a different address when booking to take advantage of this.

Choose the right time to buy your ticket.

Choose the right time to buy your ticket, as purchasing tickets on a Sunday has been proven to be cheaper. If you can only book during the week, try to do it on a Tuesday.

Fly late for cheaper prices.

Fly late for cheaper prices. Red-eye flights, the ones that leave last in the day, are typically cheaper and less crowded, so aim to book that flight if possible. You will also get through the airport much quicker at the end of the day.

PRO TIP: Get an empty water bottle with you. Once you pass the security check, fill it with water. It will save you $5

Use this APP for same day flights

The Get the Flight Out app (iOS only) from fare tracker Hopper is a go-to choice for travelers looking for same-day flights. The inventory is from major airlines as well as low-cost carriers, and the prices are always favorable. A recent search found a British Airways round-trip from JFK Airport to London's Heathrow for $300.

Take a waterproof bag

If you're travelling alone you can swim without worrying about your phone, wallet and passport laying on the beach.

You can also use it as a source of entertainment on those ultra budget flights

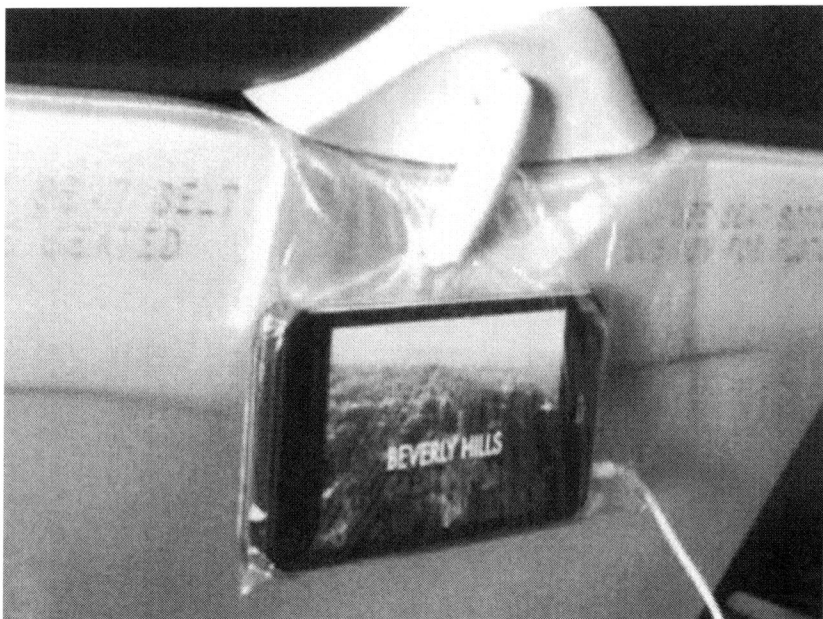

Make a private entertainment centre anywhere

Always take an eye-mask, earplugs, a scarf and a kindle reader - so you can sleep and entertain yourself anywhere!

Take a sponge with you – freeze sponges to keep your food treats fresh.

As long as they are completely frozen, you won't have any problems getting them through airport security.

Travel Gadgets

The door alarm

If you're nervous and staying in private rooms or airbnbs take a door alarm. For those times when you just don't feel safe. 'When you're in a new place, an added measure of protection can give you peace of mind to sleep.

Smart Blanket

I used it when flying to Zurich. The plane was freezing, and there were no blankets to be had. I was the only one that was warm and cozy for the whole 8 hours. Amazon http://amzn.to/2hTYlOP I paid $49.00

The coat that becomes a tent

https://www.adiff.com/products/tent-jacket

Clever Tank Top with Secret Pockets

Keep your valuables safe in this top. Perfect for all climates. https://www.amazon.com/Clever-Travel-Companion-Unisex-secret/dp/B00O94PXLE

Buy on Amazon for $39.90

Convenient Water Bottle with Built-in Pill Organizer

Great way to take your medication while on the go. The medication holder can also be detached. Holding 23 oz. or 600ml, the bottle cap also doubles as a cup. Ingenious!

Optical Camera Lens for Smartphones and Tablets

Leave your bulky camera at home. Turn your device into a high-performance camera. Buy on Amazon for $9.95

Travel-sized Wireless Router with USB Media Storage

Convert any wired network to a wireless network. Buy on Amazon for $17.99

Buy a Scrubba Bag to wash your clothes on the go

Or a cheaper imitable. You can wash your clothes on the go.

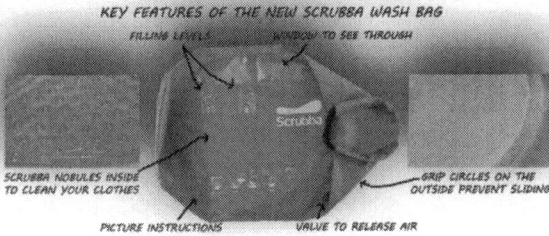

KEY FEATURES OF THE NEW SCRUBBA WASH BAG

FILLING LEVELS   WINDOW TO SEE THROUGH

SCRUBBA NOBULES INSIDE
TO CLEAN YOUR CLOTHES

GRIP CIRCLES ON THE
OUTSIDE PREVENT SLIDING

PICTURE INSTRUCTIONS   VALVE TO RELEASE AIR

On The Road

Follow locals

Follow the locals. If there are locals around you, you're doing it right. If there are only tourists, you're probably being ripped off.

Set-up a New Uber/ other car hailing app account for discounts
Google offers $50 free for new users in most cities when you have a new gmail.com email account.

Couchsurfing

Totally safe when the person has reviews, but competitive. Book early and confirm before you go. Take a tent, you'll have somewhere to stay if the host cancels last minute.

Hitch-hiking

A good option to save money on transport which will take up a much larger chunk of your budget but only do in groups and let someone know when you are at all times. Family locator app is a good way to do this automatically.

Internet

Check Foursquare for free Wi-Fi hotspots
Get a local cheap sim for data on the go.
Rewards lounges usually have unprotected Wi-Fi networks.
Buying Internet access from your mobile device rather than your laptop can get you a better rate. Alternatively, you can spoof your browser's User Agent.

Include external portable power battery for phone charging

Look for people already eating and drinking

Check the Spotted by Locals apps or blogs (Europe & North America)
Get the local experiences: Trip: The Happiest Way to Enjoy Truly Local Experiences (Trip is now available in 86 countries)

Checking Bags

Everyone says this, but it's always worth saying again: Never, ever check a bag if you possibly can avoid it. You're better off doing laundry a couple times in a hostel bathroom. You might also meet interesting people at a coin-op laundry.

Make sure to take a photo of your bag before you check it. This will speed up the paperwork if it is damaged or lost.

Take advantage of other hotel's amenities

Take advantage of other hotel's amenities, for example, if you fancy a swim but you're nowhere near the ocean, try the nearest hotel with a pool. As long as you buy a drink, the hotel staff will likely grant you access.

Fill up your mini bar for free.

Fill up your mini bar for free by storing things from the breakfast bar in your mini bar to give you a greater selection of drinks and food.

Save yourself some ironing

Save yourself some ironing by using the steam from the shower to get rid of wrinkles in clothing. If something is creased, leave it trapped with the steam in the bathroom overnight for even better results.

Recover from a big night out.

Recover from a big night out by using a pants hanger to secure the curtains, keeping your room nice and dark.

See somewhere else for free!

See somewhere else for free! Check to see if your flight offers free stopovers, allowing you to experience another city without spending any extra money.

Wear your heaviest clothes

on the plane to save weight in your suitcase, allowing you to bring more with you. Big coats can then be used as pillows to make your flight more comfortable.

Rebook for a cheaper change of flight.

Some airlines charge high changing fees, whereas last minute flights can be extremely cheap.

Google Your Flight Number before you leave for the airport

Easily find out where your plane is from anywhere. Confirm the status of your flight before you leave.

Protect your belongings during the flight.

Put a 'Fragile' on anything you check to ensure that it's handled better as it goes through security. It'll also be one of the first bags released after the flight, getting you out of the airport quicker.

Don't get lost while you're away.

Find where you want to go using Google Maps, then type 'OK Maps' into the search bar to store this information for offline viewing.

Dine Early

Walk-ins are often accommodated late in the afternoon, and reservations at buzzy restaurants are more plentiful then, too and lunch deals can be half the price of dinner.

Use car renting services

Drive Now or Car2Go.

Share Rides

Use sites like blablacar.com to find others who are driving in your direction. It can be 80% cheaper than normal transport. Just check the drivers reviews.

Use free gym passes

Get a free gym day pass by googling the name of a local gym and free day pass.

When asked by people providing you a service where you are from

If there's no price list for the service you are asking for, when asked where you are from, Say you are from a well-known poorer country. I normally say Macedonia, and if they don't know where it is, add it's a poor country. If you say UK, USA, the majority of Europe bar the well-known poorer countries taxi drivers, tour operators etc will match the price to what they think you pay at home

Hacks for Families

Rent an Airbnb apartment so you can cook

Apartments are much better for families, as you have all the amenities you'd have at home. They are normally cheaper per person too.

Shop at local markets

Eat seasonal products and local products. Get closer to the local market and observe the prices and the offer. What you can find more easily, will be the cheapest

Take Free Tours

Download free podcast tours of the destination you are visiting. The podcast will tell you where to start, where to go, and what to look for. Often you can find multiple podcast tours of the same place. Listen to all of them if you like, each one will tell you a little something new.

Pack Extra Ear Phones

If you go on a museum tour, they often have audio guides. Instead of having to rent one for each person, take some extra earphones. Most audio tour devices have a place to plug in a second set.

Free Hotel Breakfast

Only stay at hotels that include a free breakfast with their standard rate. If you are on a week-long family trip, this could save you a ton of money.

Buy Souvenirs Ahead of Time

If you are buying souvenirs someone touristy, you are paying a premium price. By ordering the same exact products online, you can save a lot of money.

Use Cheap Transportation

Do as the locals do, including weekly passes.

Carry a Reusable Water Bottle

Spending money on water and other beverages can quickly add up. Instead of paying for drinks, take some refillable water bottles.

Combine Attractions

Many major cities offer ticket bundles where one price gets you into 5 or 6 popular attractions. You will need to plan ahead of time to decide what things you plan to do on vacation and see if they are selling these activities together.

Pack Snacks

Granola bars, apples, baby carrots, bananas, cheese crackers, juice boxes, pretzels, fruit snacks, apple sauce, grapes, and veggie chips.

Stick to Carry-On Bags

Do not pay to check a large bag. Even a small child can pull a carry-on.

Visit free art galleries and museums

Just google the name + free days.

Eat Street Food

There's a lot of unnecessary fear around this. You can watch the food prepared. Go for the stands that have a steady queue.

Travel Gadgets for Families

Dropcam

Are what-if scenarios playing out in your head? Then you need Dropcam.

'Dropcam HD Internet Wi-Fi Video Monitoring Cameras help you watch what you love from anywhere. In less than a minute, you'll have it setup and securely streaming video to you over your home Wi-Fi. Watch what you love while away with Dropcam HD.'

Approximate Price: $139

Kelty-Child-Carrier

Voted as one of the best hiking essentials if you're traveling with kids and can carry a child up to 18kg.

Jetkids Bedbox

No more giving up your own personal space on the plane.

How to earn money WHILE travelling

1. Online english teaching job $20 - you will need a private room for this. - https://t.vipkid.com.cn/?refereeId=3262664
2. Work in a hostel. Normally you'll get some cash and free accommodation.
3. Fruit picking. I picked Bananas in Tully Australia for $20 an hour. The jobs are menial but can be quite meditative.
4. You could work on luxury yachts in the med. Its hard work, but you can save money - DesperateSailors.com
5. fiverr.com - offer a small service, like making a video template and changing the content for each buyer.
6. upwork.com - you need to put in a lot of work to make this successful, but if you have a unique skill like coding, or marketing it can be lucrative.
7. Make a udemy.com course
8. Use skype to deliver all manner of services, language lessons, therapy etc. Google for what you could offer. Most speclaisoms have a platform you can use to find clients and they will take a cut of your earnings/ require a fee.
9. Become an Airbnb experience host - but this requires you to know one place and stay there for a time. And you will need a work visa for that country.
10. WWOOF.org which focuses on organic farm work.
11. Rent your place out on airbnb while you travel and get a cleaner to manage it.

Safety

I always check fco.co.uk before travelling. NEVER RELY on websites or books. Things are changing constantly and the FCO's advice is always UP TO DATE and extremely conservative.

I've travelled alone to over 150 countries and the main thing I learnt is if you walk around scared, or anticipating you're going to be pickpocketed, your constant fear will attract bad energy. Murders or attacks on travellers are the mainstay of media, not reality, especially in countries familiar with travellers. The only place I had cause to genuinely fear for my life was Papa New Guinea - where nothing actually happened to me only my own panic over culture shock.

There are many things you can do to stop yourself being victim to the two main problems when travelling: theft or being scammed.

I will address theft first. Here are my top tips. Take these with a pinch of salt, I've written them whilst in India, which can be sketchy if you're travelling alone.

- Stay alert while you're out and always have an exit strategy (no alleyways when alone).
- Keep your money in a few different places on your person and your passport somewhere it can't be grabbed.
- Take a photo of your passport on your phone incase (I never lost of had mine stolen in 15 years of constant travel). If you do lose it, google for your embassy, you can usually get a temporary pretty fast.
- Google safety tips for traveling in your country to help yourself out and memorise the emergency number.
- At hostels keep your large bag in the room far under the bed/out of the way with a lock on the zipper.

- I keep all money, valuables, passport, etc on me in my day bag. And at night I keep larger bag locked and my day bag in bed next to me/under my pillow depending on how secure the rest of the facilities are. I will alter any of the above based on circumstance or comfortability, for example, the presence of lockers or how many people in the room.
- On buses/trains I would definitely have a lock on the zippers of all bags and I would even lock it to the luggage rack if you want to sleep/if this is a notoriously sketchy route. Bag theft on Indian trains for example is very common.
- I hate constantly checking my bags and having anxiety over it. I bring a small lock for all zippers (with important things not in easily accessible pockets.
- Get a personal keychain alarm. The sound will scare anyone away.
- Don't wear any jewellery. A man attempted to rob a friend of her engagement ring in Bogota, Colombia, and in hindsight I wished I'd told her to leave it at home/wear it on a hidden necklace, as the chaos it created was avoidable.
- Don't hold your phone out while in the street.
- Don't turn your back to traffic while you use your phone.
- When traveling in the tuktuk sit in the middle and keep your bag secure. Wear sunglasses as dust can easily get in your eyes.
- Watch your bag - make sure your zippers are closed and you're aware of your things.
- Don't let anyone give you flowers, bracelets, or any type of trinket, even if they insist it's for free and compliment you like crazy.
- Be careful at night & while drinking.
- Don't go solo on excursions that take you away from crowds.
- Let someone know where you are if you are fearful. Use the family app.
- Don't let strangers know that you are alone - unless they are travel friends ;-) in fact, this is more for avoiding scams or men if you are a women travelling alone.
- Lastly, and most importantly -Trust your gut! If it doesn't feel right, it isn't.

Our Writers

Phil Tang has traveled a number of places using Lonely Planet guides and finds them to be incredibly useful; however, their recommendations for restaurants and accommodation are WAY OUT of my budget. Plus any estimation of cost was always widely inaccurate. So over the past 14 years I started compiling the Super Cheap Guides guides for people like me, who want a guide within a set budget, but one that doesn't compromise on fun.

Ali Blythe has been writing about amazing places for 17 years. He loves travel and especially tiny budgets equalling big adventures nearly as much as his family. He recently trekked the Satopanth Glacier trekking through those ways from where no one else would trek. A adventure by nature and bargainist by religion, his written over 200 guides for people travelling on a budget.

Michele Whitter writes about languages and travel. What separates her from other travel writers is her will to explain complex topics in a no-nonsense, straightforward manner. She doesn't promise the world. But always delivers step-by-step strategies you can immediately implement to travel on a small Budget.

Kim Mortmier whether it's a two-week, two-month, or two-year trip, Kim's input on Super Cheap Guides Travel Guides show you how to stretch your money further so you can travel cheaper, smarter, and with more wanderlust. She loves going over land on horses.

Copyright

Published in Great Britain in 2018 by Bloom House Press LTD.

Copyright © 2018 Bloom House Press LTD.

The right of Phil G A Tang to be identified as the Author of the Work has been asserted in accordance with the Copyright, Designs and Patents Act 1988.

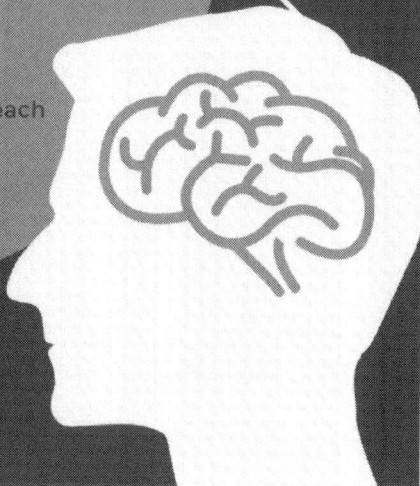

WHAT CAN WE DO BETTER?

Tell us your wishes and we'll incorporate them. We update each guide monthly.

Traveladdictguides.com

TINY BUDGET GUIDES

WHERE NEXT?

TWO WEEKS IN PERU FOR $250

TWO WEEKS IN BOLIVIA FOR $250

7 DAYS IN ENGLAND FOR $250

7V53

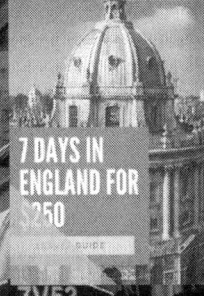

BIG EXPERIENCES FOR TINY BUDGETS.

Printed in Poland
by Amazon Fulfillment
Poland Sp. z o.o., Wrocław